The Kick-a-lot Shoes
by Joy Cowley

"I want to be mean,"
said the witch.
"Very, very mean.
What can I do?"

She looked down
at the town.

"I'll go and kick people," she said.
"That's as mean as I can get.
I'll kick them so hard that
they can't sit down."

She put on her mean old
kick-a-lot shoes.

"Here I come, all you people,"
she said.

The people looked up.
"It's the witch," they yelled.
"She's got on her kick-a-lot shoes.
Run! Run! Run!"

The witch went after the mail carrier.

"Help!" said the mail carrier.

BOOMPSA-DAISY!

The witch gave
the mail carrier a kick.

"Ow!" said the mail carrier,
and he ran away, crying.

A police officer came up to the witch.

"Now see here, Witch," he said.
"You can't kick people like that."

"Can't I?" said the witch, and
BOOMPSA-DAISY!
The kick-a-lot shoes
got the police officer, too.

"Ow!"
said the police officer,
and he ran away,
crying.

"Ha ha!"
said the witch.
"And now for that farmer."

"Help me!"
said the farmer to his cow.

"Here we go," said the witch.

BOOMPSA-DAISY!

"Ow!" said the farmer,
and he ran away, crying.

"Moo,"
said the cow.
"You kick me,
and I'll kick you."

"Is that so?"
said the witch.

BOOMPSA-DAISY!

"Moo-oo-oo," said the cow,
and it ran away, crying.

The witch went
up and down the town.

She kicked people
as they went
into their houses.
She kicked people
as they came out.

"Stop! Stop!"
said the people.
"You kicked us so hard,
we can't sit down."

But the witch
did not stop.

Then a mouse came out of
its hole in the tree.
"What's up?" it said.

It looked at the mean old witch.
It looked at the kick-a-lot shoes.
It looked at all the frightened people.

"Witch! Witch!" it said.
"You can't catch me.
You can't catch me."

Back came the kick-a-lot shoes.
The mouse ran into its hole.

BOOMPSA-DAISY!

The mean old witch kicked the tree.
"Ow!" yelled the witch.
"My foot! My foot! I can't walk!"

"Get her shoes!" yelled the people.

Off came the kick-a-lot shoes.
Off and into the river.

The broom went after them. Splash!

"My broom!" yelled the witch.
"I can't get home without my broom."

"We will help you," said the people.

"We **want** to help you,"
said the cow.

And **BOOMPSA-DAISY!**

Up went the witch.
Up, up, up, all the way to her house.

"Ow!" said the witch,
and she ran in, crying.

"What mean people," she said.
"They kicked me so hard,
I can't sit down."